Tallyessin  Silverwo

Manwaring) is a no\

(MA Teaching & Practise of Creative Writing, Cardiff University). Originally trained as an artist, he studied performance art and film on his Fine Art Degree in Coventry. He has been performing his poetry & stories for over a decade, first in Northampton, his birth town, then in venues across the Southwest (Glastonbury Festival, Bath Literature Festival, Bristol Poetry Festival etc) as well as further afield (Medieval Ball, Croydon, Royal Armouries Museum, Leeds, Rhode Island, USA.) For the passed seven years he's lived in Bath, where he's 'put down roots', planting a Celtic tree wheel, organising eco-arts events and working in community development. In 1999 he was awarded the Bardic Chair of Bath for his epic poem 'Spring Fall – the Legend of Sulis and Bladud of Bath'. With Fire Springs – Storytellers of Bath he has co-created and performed in 'Arthur's Dream' and 'Robin of the Wildwood' among others. He has been running creative-writing and performance workshops for all ages since establishing Tallyessin Training in 2000 with a Prince's Trust Loan. He has worked with, and performed for, primary school children to senior citizens. In 2003 he edited 'Writing the Land – an anthology of natural words,' after receiving a Reading Families Millennium Award. He has written 7 collections of poetry and 3 novels; 'The Ghost Tree', 'The Sun Miners' and 'The Long Woman'. He currently runs Way Of Awen Development – a year-long bardic training programme, and teaches creative writing for the Open University.

Dedicated to the spirit of Taliesin Pen Beirdd

May his name never die

And his poetry always live.

I walk with awe in the footsteps of giants.

/|\

AWEN

# GREEN

# FIRE

MAGICAL VERSE

FOR THE

WHEEL OF THE YEAR

BY

Tallyessin Silverwolf

©2004

First published in Great Britain by *Awen Publications* 2004,
The Cauldron, 7 Dunsford Place, Bath BA2 6HF

www.tallyessin.com  Email:awen@tallyessin.com

A CIP record for this book is available from the British Library.

ISBN 0-9546137-3-2

All artwork by *Kevan Manwaring* copyright 2004

**CREDITS**

Poems previously published (under the name Kevan Manwaring):

*The Bride of Spring, Summer's Wake:* Remembrance Days Imp Press 1991
*Merry Maiden, Maid Flower Bride, One With The Land:* Gramarye Imp Press 1995
*Solace of Sulis, Awakening the King:* Spring Fall, Imp Press 1998
*The Creation of Taliesin, Child of Everything, Blessed is the Mother, Wheel of the Rose, Ancestral Mariner, Wild Hunt:* Immrama, Imp Press 1999
*Enchantment of Merlin:* Arthur's Dream – story CD with Fire Springs, Abaris 2001
*The Wicker Man, Heartwood, The Prophets of Los:* Waking the Night Imp Press 2002
*Wolf in the City, Your Love, Praise Song for Glastonbury:* The Hole Magazine #3 2003

Extract in introduction from '*A Sand County Almanac*' by Aldo Leopold from What is Deep Ecology? Stephen Harding, Resurgence no.185, 1997

Printed in Valhalla & Garamond

Printed and bound by Parchment the Printers

Printworks, Crescent Road, Cowley, Oxford OX4 2PB
Email:print@parchmentUK.com
www.PrintUK.com Tel: 01865 747547

# CONTENTS                                    PAGE

## ILLUSTRATIONS
(by Kevan Manwaring unless otherwise stated)

1. Horned God, oils, front cover.
2. Wheel of the Year, graphic, by Sheila Broun, p9
3. AND, oils, p15
4. Cathy with waif at Wessex Gathering, photograph by author p17
5. Shining Brow, ink, p19
6. Child of Light, ink, p21
7. Sulis, oils, p23
8. GlobaLove, watercolours, p24
9. Watersmeet, watercolours, p26
10. Shadowdance, oils, p28
11. Goddess, ink, gouache, pencil, p30
12. White Horse, ink, p32
13. Cerne Abbas, ink, p33
14. Rivals, ink, p40
15. Flower Bride, oils, p41
16. Moondancing, oils, p44
17. Amesbury Archer, photograph by Marie Leverett, p49
18. Stonehenge, ink, p51
19. Men-an-tol, ink, p55
20. Manannan, linocut, p56
21. Manawyddan, watercolours, p58
22. Newgrange, ink, p65
23. Llew, oil pastels, p68
24. Long Man, ink, p69
25. Light in the Trees, oil pastels, p75
26. Lord of the Dead, inks, p77
27. Oak growing out of Rock, ink, p80
28. Wolf Howl, oils, p81
29. Burning Man, ink, p85
30. Springhead, ink, oil pastels, p90
31. Stoney Littleton, ink, oil pastels, p91
32. Bladud Head, oils, p94
33. Tor, ink, p97
34. Shining Word, graphic, p100
35. Green Man, oils, back cover.

# INTRODUCTION

Celebrate the turning of the wheel with this collection of bardic verse. It is based upon my repertoire as a performer and has developed over thirteen years. Each one of these poems I perform from memory, in the bardic tradition. They were written from the heart, composed for the ear, and edited by the tongue. I suggest you try the same approach. In learning our words by heart we can speak from the soul and not from a piece of paper – the performance becomes immediately more powerful and personal, audience awareness increases as eye contact can be maintained, and the audience's respect for the poet is heightened, because the performer has made an effort. When we speak with love and sincerity we truly shine.

I have used these poems to create a magical mood, to sanctify, and to raise energy. They are invocations and blessings – ways of honouring the gods, our sacred times and places, and ourselves.

The title of this anthology comes from a quote by Aldo Leopold, wildlife manager and ecologist, who had a Damascus-like experience once while hunting in the Twenties:

> One morning, Leopold was out with some friends on a walk in the mountains. Being hunters, they carried their rifles with them, in case they got a chance to kill some wolves. It got around lunch-time, and they sat down on a cliff overlooking a turbulent river. Soon they saw what appeared to be some deer fording the torrent, but they soon realised was a pack of wolves. They took up their rifles and began to shoot excitedly into the pack, but with little accuracy. Eventually an old wolf was down by the side of the river, and Leopold rushed down to gloat at her death.

What met him was a fierce green fire dying in the wolf's eyes. He writes in a chapter entitled Thinking like a Mountain that: "there was something new to me in those eyes, something known only to her and to the mountain. I thought that fewer wolves meant more deer, that no wolves would mean hunter's paradise. But after seeing the green fire die, I sensed that neither the wolf nor the mountain agreed with such a view."

Changed by his experience, Leopold became a great ambassador for wilderness, a writer of the wild. I have had similar (but less dramatic and damaging!) experiences with nature – yet my revelation was incremental, as I slowly became aware of the green fire in all living things. My daily childhood rambles, walking my dog, turned me into a pagan and a poet of the planet. I found my words in the woods first, and later in books. An image from the 13th Century Welsh collection The Mabinogion captures for me the haunting dream-like quality of Celtic myth that has so inspired me ever since:

On the bank of the river he saw a tall tree: from roots to crown one half was aflame and the other green with leaves.

This is the green fire of the imagination, Dylan Thomas's 'the force that through the green fuse drives the flower.' Nature's majesty and mystery lit my fuse. Through my words I aspire to honour that which gives me life, meaning and joy. I hope you enjoy them. Perhaps they will inspire you to write your own to celebrate the annual cycle. By harmonising with nature we no longer harm it.

May the green fire never die!

*Tallyessin Silverwolf* / | \

# THE WHEEL OF THE YEAR
### by Sheila Broun

SAMHAIN - marks the beginning of winter and the Celtic New Year. A time of death and rebirth – the fruit has decayed and the seed is left, holding the pattern of next year's cycle.

YULE - celebrates the turning point of the sun at midwinter. From this time onwards, light increases. Frost spreads across the land and everything is strengthened through rest.

IMBOLC - here are the first stirrings of life. Shoots of the first flowers come through the earth. The early lambs are born, and the cockerel joins the hens and they begin to lay again.

SPRING EQUINOX - day and night are of equal length. A time to celebrate the beauty of dawn. The earth is awake and seeds germinate and burst into life. The mating season begins.

BELTANE - marks the beginning of summer. This is the merry month of May when everything blossoms. It is a time of fertility and rapid growth.

SUMMER SOLSTICE - a time of maximum light and the longest day of the year. A time to enjoy golden summer days. From this time onwards the light decreases.

LAMMAS - first fruits of harvest. A time of abundance and celebration. A time of giving thanks to the earth for our food, and of working together.

AUTUMN EQUINOX - day and night are of equal length again. The harvest is finally gathered in with thanksgiving. A time to celebrate the beauty of dusk.

# BLESSINGS OF THE SILVER BRANCH

Bright salutations on this merry company,
High blessings to our generous host,
And peace to the spirits of this place.

I am Tallyessin the Bard
of Caer Badon, Caer Abiri and Cor Gawr,
and I come to you in this hall, at this hour.

I wield the silver branch,
Ancient sign of my craft,
Wise key to the Otherworld.

As the Queen of Elfland's bell-strewn reign
Aeneas' bough, the Apple Tree of Emain,
May it guide you there, and back again.

Come with me and taste the apples of Awen.
One bite will bestow wisdom and inspiration,
Like three drops from the cauldron of Ceridwen.

Memory of animals be mine,
wisdom of ancestors be mine.
In the name of the God and the Goddess,
Grant me your grace – let the brow shine!

# EXILES

Once in Arcadia we did belong

and to its music dwelled in harmony.

Now in discord we dance to a duller song.


Forgotten, secret name of flower, tree,

broken the first friendships of man's childhood.

Bird and egg have become a mystery.


Strangers now to the familiar wood,

where once we wandered we have lost our way.

Mud, litter and din mark where we have trod.


Our wild cousins beware and will not play,

for heavy footfalls wait, alert to dart.

For human greed they have been made to pay.


It is from this family we chose to part,

yet can return - by the paths of the heart.

## PAGAN CREED

*I am a pagan,*
I belong to the world.
*I am a pagan,*
Gaia's love child.
*I am a pagan,*
Green Man stirs my blood.
*I am a pagan,*
I worship in the wildwood.

The Earth is my temple,
The planet it is sacred.
I honour what sustains me,
By the feast of life I'm fed.

For those who've gone before,
And those yet to be,
Let's leave this world better,
Fertile, safe and free.

The two-legged, the four-legged,
Feathered, finned and furred.
The tiniest to the mightiest.
May they all be heard.

*I am a Pagan, I am a Pagan*

In my magic harming none,
So let me work my will.
Walking paths by other names,
We can be brothers still.

*I am a Pagan, I am a Pagan.*

By the seasons of the sun,
And the cycles of the moon,
By starlight, twilight and dawn.
By sygyl, ogham and rune.
I take my vow, never break my vow,
That Heaven is here and now!

*I am a Pagan, I am a Pagan.*
Heathen, wiccan, druid, priests high –
All pagans under one sky.

*I am a Pagan,*
By spiral paths I roam,
*I am a Pagan.*
Finally coming home.

*I am Pagan,*
Find me by my star.
Coven, moot, grove and clan,
The Gods know who you are!

# IMBOLC

# The Bride of Spring

In darkest hour of the year
she arises.
Casting off her shadowy gown
as she steps over the horizon –
by sun king kissed,
borne by his golden down.
A dress of frosted cobwebs
veils maiden skin.
Within a seasons turning
the crone has become virgin.
Snowdrops touch her and turn into flowers,
as the slumbering land stirs
in these formative hours.
The earth softens at her feet
where buds shake free their winter bed.
Newborn lambs begin to bleat –
insistent mouths by ewes milk fed.
Rooster heralds her on the ground.
Above, the feathered chorus
make naked trees resound.

We awake to a changing world.
Her white magic revealed -
a petal uncurled.

Stone bound man
let your proud bells ring,
for we are welcomed into her garden
as she stand at the gates of spring.

The infant year she presents,
placing the future in our hands.
A gift of renewed innocence,
restoring the egg timer sands...

# The Song of Taliesin

I hail from the realm of the summer stars -
I am the living memory of Merlin.
My lord, Elffin, caught me in a weir -
His bard I became: behold, Taliesin.

Yet this is but one branch of my ancestry –
Before I was a boy as old as history...

I have been a mountain hare, crazy-eyed, tail high,
I have been a wise salmon swimming up stream,
I have been the king of the birds, catching sky,
I have been a wheaten seed of golden gleam –
Swallowed into the belly of the Black Hen.
By White Sow reborn,
a helpless babe on a boundless sea –
Deep waters where I was also the wind's shadow,
The wrathful wave upon promontory.

My eyes are the fiery tears of the sun,
My Muse from the Moon Queen's Cauldron.

Poetry is my spear,
I am a warrior of words!
I know the lays of this land
And the language of birds,
The tongue of stone

And the song of trees
And the forest of your families.

I know the first name of constellations,
The blessed ancestors
And the Undying Ones.

I was born when the world was still in womb,
I shall be with humanity 'til the crack of doom.
Proud kingdoms I have seen ebb and flow,
Their glory I have sung and echoed their woe.

My curriculum vitae is universal and timeless,
I am the quicksilver serpent of the Caduceus.
By fire and fur and feather and scale,
I, Taliesin, bid thee hail!

# The Child of Everything

*I am the Child of Everything -*
*do not play with my fire!*
*I defy your modifications -*
*mutations not in isolation -*
*their consequences will be dire...*

I am as old as creation,

I am the genius of genesis,

I am the seed of paradise,

I am the dancing serpent-twin,

I am the fruit of knowledge,

I am the sap of the world tree,

I am the pulse of the planet's heart,

I am in everything under the sun.

*I am the Child of Everything –*
*(Chorus)*

I am the grit in the oyster,

I am the gleam in your ancestor's eye,

I am the quick of the dead,

I am the dew on the divine web,

I am the spawn in the gene pool,

I am the fingerprints of parents,

I am the pollen on the breeze,

I am the eye of the storm.


*I am the Child of Everything -*

*do not play with my fire!*

*I defy your modifications -*

*mutations not in isolation -*

*Their consequences will be dire.*

# The solace of Sulis

Weary traveller
        find sanctuary near.
Leave the false flow behind ~
take a walk down Bridewell Lane
to the threshold of the White Doorway.

Enter with gentle feet:
  for here life flowers from the cracked earth.
Hush and hark the magic gush.
Watch the wise waters rise
  that fell as rain a hundred centuries ago...

As though the ancient thoughts
        of a dormant giant
    bubbles aspire to the air,
  steam dreams ascend
        to a sky of wings.

Scry the swirling mist:
see what manifests...
Gaze into the eyes of the Goddess:
    deep green pools
        wherein dwells;

arcane knowledge;

bountiful fertility;

immortal beauty.

To the triple fountainhead of

cronemothermaiden

place your offerings.

Rekindle the temple flame

and honour She-with-a-thousand-names

who heals and inspires

with her sacred cauldron.

*Deae Suli*

*Blessed Be*

# SPRING EQUINOX

# The wheel of the rose

From the ocean of the heart let Venus rise:
See her dawning in your lover's eyes.
In sighing chest she cannot hide,
Flow to the rhythm of her tide.

Follow her seasons about the earth -
Who weathers them all will prove their worth.
Through weal and woe true love learns -
Thus the wheel of the rose turns.

Who can say when love begins?
It is a circle that always spins -
Around and around it our lives rotate,
Repeating the past is often our fate.

The arrows of Eros will be your thorn,
Until you worship Aphrodite's throne.
Offer yourself: mind, body and soul,
And she will heal you and make you whole.

Water this rose with the dew of your tears
And it will blossom all of your years.
Share this chalice with humanity,
And your life will be filled with harmony.

## YOUR LOVE

Your love is a mountain of faith,
It is my pillar to heaven,
My moveable temple -
I take sanctuary in it,
It nourishes me.

Waters meet

Your love gives me the strength to live my truth.
Armed with your belief
I can accomplish anything.

Your love is my oceanwind,
My guiding star.
It is a proud ship, it is waves breaking.
Your love fills my sails, lifts my flags.

It is the air that feeds my candle flame,
It is the light and it is the darkness,
The night that soothes,
A nest of dreams.

Your love is being embraced by your eyes,
Being seen by your lips, tasted by your hands.
Your love is a feast, A dinner prepared with tenderness,
A blessed transformation.

Your love is an act of grace,
A redemption and a release.
It is a prayer and an offering,
A flower that will never wilt.

Your love is a soft rain,
It is a song sung in silence.
I am listening to it now,
The endless syllable between the words.

I float upon it in my sleep.
Waking, I wear it like a cloak,
An invisible cloak.

And walk with it protected –

An angel at my shoulder

Taking me home

# Blessed is the Mother

Blessed is the Mother -
honour Her on your day of birth.
Sacred is the Mother -
whose body is this precious Earth.

Find Her in the bend of a brook,
in the song of a secret spring.
Feel Her in a verdant vale,
in the joy of nature's flowering.

Follow Her contours in the curved breast of a mound,
in the swollen belly of a hill.
Face Her in the fertile tomb of barrow womb,
in the dark and silence and still.

*Mater Tierra, Prima Mater.*

Earth Warriors, rise up!
Defend your Motherland.
The Dogs of Babylon
bite Her fair hand.

Mothers of the Future,
may your hearts be true -
tomorrow's generation
all depends on you.

Blessed is the Mother
of all Creation great and small-
Planet, animal, man and God:
the Mother Universal!

*Mater Tierra, Prima Mater.*
*Mater Tierra, Prima Mater.*

## BIRDS OF RHIANNON

From a high hill
you can see her coming -
riding along the bridal ways.
Wife of the Underworld
astride a white mare
and veiled in gold.

Try as you may
you will not catch her -
unless she wants to catch you.
The reins of your heart
are in her hands -
she's a wild wind from distant lands.

*Hear the Birds of Rhiannon;*
*Under their spell time will slow…*
*O the Birds of Rhiannon;*
*Forget your head and heartache let go…*

Listen to her story –
she can carry you to court
and make you a king.
The Queen of Annwvyn on
her steed of sovereignty.
She has all you need in her bag of plenty.

Anxieties nurse – she will heal your burden.

As all mothers she's had to suffer.

Pale muse, dream rider -

her groom was Manawyddan.

See her horses come ashore –

she's the Bride of the Ocean.

*Hear the Birds of Rhiannon;*

*Under their spell time will slow…*

*O the Birds of Rhiannon;*

*Forget your head and heartache let go…*

Ride on, ride on, Rhiannon…

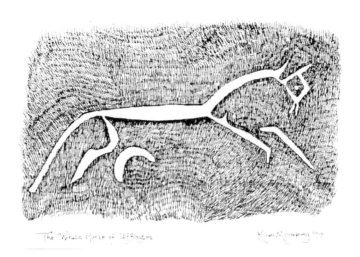

The White Horse of Uffington

# BELTANE

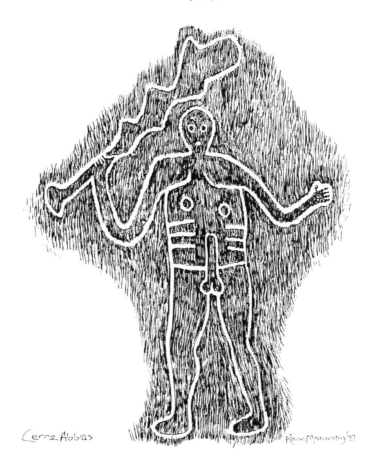

Cerne Abbas

## MERRY MAIDEN

I dreamt last of Merry Maiden...
She had faery ring fingers and bluebell shoes.
Waking, I still wished I was dreaming
As I asked everywhere what nobody knows.
I said;

*Have you seen my merry maiden?*
*She danced all night in*
*Moonfields of dreams.*
*I long to find my merry maiden –*
*She sang to me sweet:*
*'Nothing's what it seems...'*

Meandering down mermaid lanes,
crawling across cromlech moors,
teetering between crack and crag
'til my feet and heart were sore.

To the end of the land
I vowed to chase her –
From the first to the last
Of old England.

In the hawthorn blossom
Did I see her flower hair –
Her golden brow in the shifting sand?

Did I catch her scent
In the pisky wood –
Called to the secret cove,
Or amongst the thorns and mud
As all day and night I madly roved?

[Chorus]

Well, the preacher man called her a tempting demon.
The wise woman a faery leman.
Yet, whatever she's called I yearn to find her –
My many-faced merry maiden.


Was she just a figment of my imagination?
The product of a fevered mind?
Sprite of fancy or soul companion –
She was my Golden Hind.


The rain lashed down when the sun didn't cinder.
I staggered through dark night and cold.
But come Hell or high water, I knew I must woo her
Like a knight on a quest of old.


[Chorus]


Alas, the journey wound on and on,
Grey skies did obscure my goal…
Yet if we lose sight of our vision
Then we risk losing our soul.

I needed shelter from the storm,
'til those clouds of unknowing had passed;
a place dry, warm and welcoming...
All I had to do was ask.

I should've known - home's where the heart is.
My destination was my haven.
Suddenly it dawned on me – she was there all along,
My familiar merry maiden.

She took my aching hand,
Soothed my weary brow,
Saying with a kiss
It'll all work out somehow.

At last!
Together with my merry maiden –
All I ever needed was you.
You're the sweet truth faery,
Surely living proof – a fey dream come true!

*Merry, merry, merry maiden-*
*She led me up the path to her garden.*
*Merry, merry, merry maiden –*
*She is the stuff that dreams are made on.*

*Merry, merry, merry maiden...*

# The Winning of Spring

*Adapted from Culhwch & Olwen, The Mabinogion.*

This is the ballad of a fatal lady –
The fairest in the land,
Her name was Creiddylad,
Daughter of Nudd Silverhand.

Her hair was like a river,
Her eyes as bright as morn.
O, how she danced in that green, green dress –
Elusive as the dawn.

Yet there was a fool who would woo her –
A gentle knight named Gwythyr.
He set out over the mountain
In search of her sweet favour.

He came upon a screaming mound:
It was a burning ant-hill.
Quickly, he saved it and the occupants said
'May we one day save you from peril!'

Well, Gwythyr recalled Culhwch –
No less than Arthur's first cousin,
Who was trying to win the hand of Olwen –
Daughter of the dread giant Ysbaddeden.

One of Culhwch's many tasks was to collect
Nine thousand grains of linseed...
Gwythyr's little army obliged
And so returned his good deed.

When old Nudd heard of this noble knight
He thought him a suitable suitor.
Creiddylad was not so keen –
But she had little say in the matter.

Yet the day was never to come
That she so haughtily dreaded.
For another was to take her first:
Kidnapped at night by Gwynn ap Nudd.

The Dark Lord on his dark horse
Swept her back to a glass isle within.
Here he kept her prisoner, declaring:
'You are now my bride – welcome to Ynis Wytryn!'

When Gwythyr got wind of this
He was most wondrously wrath.
Gathering his war-band he declared:
'For his wedding gift I shall give him his death!'

Alas, Gwynn was no mere mortal;
For he dwelled among the dead.

So when they met in battle
It was not his blood that was shed.


Many valiant warriors rode into the frey
And many there did fall.
Of Gwythyr's men none escaped but he:
Any prisoners were treated cruel.


Among there number were Nwython and son,
Who was known thereafter as Kyledr the Wild.
The father was slain, his heart cut out
And fed to son beguiled.


Kyledr went wildly mad
And so nearly did Gwythyr with grief –
For he had lost many brothers-in-arms,
As well as his erstwhile wife.


Yet Gwythyr was a goodly man
Who did not deserve such calamity.
So when the King heard of his plight
He set forth with a remedy.


Arthur's own knights came to the aid
Of he who helped Royal cousin.
The bravest and the best lay siege
To the fortress of Annwvyn.

Nothing could withstand the righteous might
Of Pendragon's shining company.
The Dark Lord finally surrended
And what prisoners were left set free.

Thus Gwynn ap Nudd did not get his bride –
But neither did poor Gwythyr,
For Arthur decreed it wisest
That she returned to her father.

'There shall never be peace here
whilst Creiddylad remain
innocent of this slaughter she may be
but she has been the root of much pain.

'Thus, to cease others suffering
For her heart's consent,
I, Arthur Pendragon,
Now do pass this final judgement:

'Every year duel for your beloved
on the first of merry May…
until the end of time itself,
when the victor will win his prize
on the very last day.'

# MAID FLOWER BRIDE

*Blodeuwedd, Guinevere, Marion, Niamh,*
*Blodeuwedd, Guinevere, Marion, Niamh,*
*Blodeuwedd, Guinevere, Marion, Niamh...*

Step within the golden grove
And you may see a maid so green –
In a world of her own devising
Where all time and truth is seen.

41

Naked as the day, I saw her,
Her spirit as a new sunrise.


Glowing, knowing, shining brightly –
A sight so rich for soul sore eyes.


The beatitude of her being
stunned me into still silence -
the magic of her majesty
as I was graced by her presence.


*Woodland, lake and moon-glade lady –*
*Hail, fair queen of all Faerie!*
*Enchantress, muse, and woman wisely -*
*Ageless one who is all three.*


Unfolding, a face of flowers,
Lily nape and snowdrop skin.
Heady bouquet of her bower,
Orchid neck, buttercup chin.


Hidden pollen always luring
In her eyes of iris's at dawn –
Petals perpetually blooming
'neath eyebrows knitted with roses thorn.


Stymen lashes, catkin lobes,
With lips like split strawberries.

Picking cherry, chewing pith,
And licking tongue of hive honey.

*Woodland, lake and moon-glade lady –*
*Hail, fair queen of all Faerie.*
*Enchantress, muse, and woman wisely -*
*Ageless one who is all three.*

Peach fur of thigh and forearm,
Dusky scent of her passing.
Smooth apples of her bosom
Breathlessly ripening.

Cleaving to proud husk of hips,
Lunar shyness of her brow,
Ivy entwined into locks,
Slender sapling, supple bough.

Dancing fronds of her fingers,
Tender roots of tendril toes,
Whatever they must surely cling to
Only her smiling answer knows.

*Woodland, lake and moon-glade lady –*
*Hail, fair queen of all Faerie.*
*Enchantress, muse, and woman wisely -*
*Ageless one who is all three.*

Under her nectared navel

A warm moss crevice can be gleaned –

A spring inside, a sacred cradle,

From whence all life is wheaned.


An endless well, forever thirsty,

Whose healing heart is so deep.

Rejuvernating, never empty,

And grave secrets it always keeps.


All I am is thanks to your, ma'am –

Wholeheartedly you do possess.

Tempter, lover, mother, teacher,

Blessed be, forever Goddess!

## One with the Land

I come in many guises,
John Barleycorn and Puck.
Want to find me, pilgrim?
All you have to do is look.

Close your eyes and think of Albion,
Spin around and call my name -
Y'know, the one who shies from neon,
But is of ancient global fame...

Who?

*The Green Man -*
*I grow therefore I am.*
*The Green Man -*
*Adam naming Eden.*

I've been around since times began
And I may have lent a hand,
Y'see, my forte is creation-
Making real what She has planned.

In the caves I became the shaman
With totem, hide and drum.
Inspired them with the spark of fire,

Fan their dreams to become human.


With Buddha under the Bodhi Tree
And monkey on a cloud.
To Gilgamesh I was Enkidu -
I died to be wild.


Down in Egypt I was Osiris,
Greenskinned consort to the Queen.
Torn from serpent to the stars,
There's nowhere I haven't been.


Don't panic when you hear me
Going wild with my pipes.
Scapegoated as Satan,
But that was mostly sour grapes.


One thing the Romans and Greeks agreed -
I was the God of wine.
Bacchus or Dionysus,
You still see me on pub signs,


_Because I'm the Green Man_
_And foliage frequents my face._
_The Green Man,_
_Nature's saving grace._


The Celts called me Cernunnos,

Carried me far in their cauldron.

Druids invoked my dragon power

In oaken temples to the sun.


From Taliesin tales to Merlin,

King Arthur to Robin Hood

And begetting around the Bel-fire

I was the Witches' God.


Alas, the Puritans tried to burn me,

Victorians categorise.

Yet no matter how they smother me

My sap will always rise.


With my horn of plenty

I can give you something organic!

Feast on the fruit of planet

without ingredient genetic.


Go on, get your hands dirty,

Our Goddess is in peril.

This land's our garden - can you dig it?

It's a matter of survival!


*Says I, the Green Man,*

*Ambassador of Earth.*

*The Green Man*

*And I'm dying for rebirth.*

Who?

*Robin Goodfellow*

Who is?

*Jack-in-the-Green*

Who is one?

*Green Knight*

Who is one with?

*Pan?*

Who is one with the?

*Horned God*

Who is one with the land?


*The Green Man*


*The Green Men*

*The Green Women*

*The Green Children*


WE are one with the land.

We are one with land.

We are one with the land.

# HEART WOOD

The arrow's loosed, the chase is done,
Dappled bushes, buds unfold,
The wand is split, the garland won,
Unlocking hoard of summer gold.

*In the heartwood you wooed me,*
*In the heartwood, under trysting tree.*

Eglantine and apple blossom,
Meadowsweet and Maytree white,
Spring is awakening in the wildwood,
Life returning after winter's night.

*In the heartwood you wooed me,*
*In the heartwood, under trysting tree.*

With the dew the sap is rising,
Scented petals release their spell,
Robin's with Marian in his bower,
Honeysuckle and bluebell.

*In the heartwood you wooed me,*
*In the heartwood, under trysting tree.*

The leaves are yearning for the sunshine,
The glade echoes with mating call,
For the rain the thirsty roots pine,
Love, the huntress, has us in her thrall.

*In the heartwood you wooed me,*
*In the heartwood, under trysting tree.*

When we love the world it gladdens,
Leaf and fruit, milk and stream,
Faerie magic is all around us,
May we never awaken from this dream.

*In the heartwood, Robin and Marian,*
*In the heartwood, we are one...*

# SUMMER SOLSTICE

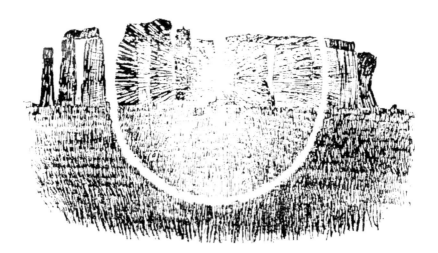

# IN THE NAME OF THE SUN

Born from the briefest night, the longest day,
The dream of winter becomes summer light.
Eyes to the East, we wait from dark to bright.
Our lord to awake, with drum breath we pray.
Gathered in this free grove of Awen's way
Robed, skyclad, blade, stave - all one in his sight.
Hail, noon of the year, the sun at its height.
Furthest North, farthest to fall – for pride, pay.

For today our King's enemy appears,
A shadow marrs his glorious parade.
Oak's usurper, holly sharpens his spears.
After this zenith the splendour shall fade.
Let us revel in his generous gaze
Blessed by the summer sun's bountiful ways.

# PRAISE SONG FOR A LOST FESTIVAL

## 1

### Sun

Oak summer sun - it's Glasters again!

The clans are gathering

in the dragon field, goblin market, canvas city, freak economy –

rainbowgnomepixiepunk. Gandalf hats, flamenco frills –

buy the latest festival victim junk.

Veggie Burgers & herbal pills from Babylon Street at Pilton.

Mixing desk, pyramid stage –

you fail to rendezvous,

but you bump into old friends and make some new.

Seasoned veterans making merry,

festival virgins lose their cherry.

Kids take the madness in their stride.

Look! Naked loonies in a mudslide.

Lost sprogs, clogs & dogs,

dropping your torch down the bogs.

Flags rippling, tipis and turbines,

crystal healing and cosmic leylines.

Watching the world do its thing,

within the steel crust-proof ring.

Fellowship of the trip,

surfing the strands of the dream-catcher maze,

floating the good vibes, the ambient haze.

Banging their drum, nailing their colours to the mast,

timeless mandalas that will not last - a vision of a dream

came true. Finishing the manuscript of Xanadu.

## 2

### Moon

Fractal cloud sunset,

an oboe and kora duet.

Everything is gilded so we don't forget.

Gold leaf patina,

light-spinner, air-juggler.

The city of lights wink on -

the night of earthly delights has  begun,

and the punters start shining.

Thank God Glastonbury's back on!

Eavis with flowers, quoting Tennyson.

A topless French girl recites a mermaid poem in German.

Everybody having *that* Glastonbury highlight;

the best band you have ever seen in a marquee

*somewhere* in the middle of the night.

If only you could remember their name, your name,

where your tent is...

Status: certainly not *compos mentis.*

Countless connections and misdirections.

Chasing the moon lady, looking-glass wizards,

weird visions, glimpses of Avalon.

A million memories flashing and the faerie city's  gone.

Leaving a harvest of tat,

random footwear, abandoned ransacked tents,

some treasure in the rubbish,

mixed in with the human mud,

and just some dazed cows chewing the cud.

# Lughnasadh

Men an-tol, Cornwall    11 August 1977    Kevan Manwaring

## ANCESTRAL MARINER

When night and the day are one
He travels the Silver Road –
The moon's shattered mirror –
Riding his white-crested stallion.

Rising from the last wave, becloaked
in the dyes of its myriad weave,
nets of bladderwrack tinkling with shells,
magic branch of driftwood helping his sea legs ashore.

Drenched in his father's sweat,
With seaweed mane
And sun-bleached beard
And salty scent of his element.

Grey eyes gleaming fathomlessly
Of fabled islands,
Sunken kingdoms,
And leviathans.

*Manannan, Manawyddan,*
*Ogham tongue, ocean son...*

Bringing the future from the horizon,
he is the giver of vision.
His ship is thought,
Answers are his sword.

Within his sack of crane-skin
He carries the poet's hoard.
At high-tide it flows to the brim –
When low its treasures are lacking.

Constant ceaseless, ever fecund,
Listen to its flowing song,
Lines from the deep tenderly pulling
To where your heart belongs.

Whispering roar

Echoing your heart's desire,

Soothing heart storms

With the thrumming of his lyre.


*Manannan, Manawyddan,*

*Ogham tongue, ocean son...*

# LAST RITES FOR JOHN BARLEYCORN

Twilighters,
Roam with me...

Through the Gates of Herne
To find a kernel of truth,
Confront the stag of the seventh tine,
Decode the marks of his horned hoof.

Down the familiar paths we trod,
Frequenting our earlier selves;
Sharing our picnic of the past –
Feasting with Pooka and his Elves.

Then over the bloodstream
And through the iron turnstiles,
Two into one –
Led by the Maiden of the Corn
To the barrow to be reborn.

Along a tunnel to the light –
Spurred on sperm, a wheaten worm,
Wisely upstream wriggling.
To germinate where we are but a gleam
-   Prodigal suns returning.

Walking between the worlds,
Through fields of alien wheat,
To the place of hallowed dreams,
Where all our tomorrows meet.

Rising to that yawning cleft;
Between that baked earth, right,
And bearded barley, ripe –
Beyond all that is left.

Demeter mourns for her lost youth,
Russet cloak unleavening
The burgeoning Lammas-scape
In her widowed wake.

Yet, if she lifted up her downcast eyes
They would glimpse a gladdening light
That could demystify those
Night-stung tears of dew.

Rekindle a faltering love
Which was once so bright;
Tinderbox heart sparked ablaze
By this Promethean view.

Look! His dazzling smile already melts
Her frosty gaze –
The heartening land smiles welcome

As the colour returns to her cheeks.


With a God's eye view
We discerned the canvas
Upon which he painted -
Pigments selected from a divine palette,
Sable-soaked, laden with morning hue -
As elegantly across the vast vista
He swept it.


Drowsy textures arose -
Dormant tints, awoken by his touch.
As our orbs imperceptibly peeled
An earthairfirewater colour
Was unveiled.


Rich vermillions, sombre umbers,
Occult ochres, verdant viridians,
Were presented by this prismatic parade
As if such a spectrum had never before
Dared to emerge from the shade.


Blinded by an unearthly faith,
We now rubbed our eyes
At this dawning creation
With a renewed belief.


Breathtaken, we breathed it back:

Pulling the sky towards us
In lungfuls of light –
Then exhaling,
The clouds dispelled like dandelions.

An impromptu pantheon,
Recreating the world
In our own fractured image.
Raise an eyebrow to influence the air,
Lift a finger and the crops would soar,
Invert a thumb and harvests fail…

But who are we to judge,
When from afar, we appear mere
Dot-to-dots,
Yearning for a common thread?

Yet the lionheart's golden mane
Is not ours to wantonly flay;
Braided bails of spiralling corn
The only evidence
Of a God that passed this way.

Now hush - for fields have ears
And silence is as golden as the sun.

From the dancing trees
Our forest kith could be heard;

Amongst the bustling stalks
The flower kin spread the word.

It was a choral dawn like no other –
The morning eavesdropped upon by Adam
when first he emerged from the
All-Mother.

A myriad of voices chattered away,
But in the same tongue spoken.
Revealed! The lost language of the fey
- our ears had awoken!

The gloaming star winked green:
It knew a secret – we did not.
The champion waited for
Was finally seen, borne in his sacred cot.

*Lugh! He soars by bronzed chariot.*
*Lugh! He strums with a solar lyre.*
*Lugh! He sings with honey lyric.*
*Lugh! He sees through eyes of fire.*

We toasted the rising king
With wide eyes and barley wine,
Our joy expressed in sundancing –
Jumping alive with ecstatic mime.

Lost in the landscape of Lughnasadh,

The moment telescoping,

Outside time.


It was ourselves looking at our elves,

which the Outsiders insighted –

a frame within a frame.

The burning gallery ignited.


Rocketed by déjà vu (again)

A product of eternal combustion,

This glimpse of infinity's spark?


For the answer to that endless question

We had to go where none return:

Down amongst the dead men,

Hoping in the dark.


Skull walls leered in silent mockery,

A sarcophagus whistled

A deadly tune;

Lulled, rolling into the barrow,

Returning to the tomb…

Way, way down there:
A rag, a bone, a hank of hair –
Would that be all that is left
To resurrect us?

O Lazarus,  O Lazarus.

Ashes to – what then – Ashes?

Dust to – nothing more than – Dust?

As cold clay kissed awake,
Mannequins of the Fire Drake.

Charged in this earthen kiln,
Ossified, lacquered and brittle,

Until dropped, and shattered

At the marriage of the Quick and the Dead.

Each shard indicative

Of the punishment or pleasure

Stretching ahead..?

No,

Not whilst friends remain

To keep one's memory alive -

Though tempests torment us,

Storms in our cracked cup.

Join hands

and we will endure.

The dead talked

Amongst themselves;

Thick as thieves –

They kept their secrets,

We kept our lives.

For now we had descended

To the summit's peak,

Casting our reflections

Upon the waters of the deep.

It was time to go,

To leave a votive offering behind.

Confronted,
The past's shadow was exchanged
For something of worth to find.

The sacred place resanctified,
By rites of passage outworn,
We emerged remembered,
Reconciled, reborn.

Crawling blinking into the brightening world,
We learnt to see again, through fields of vision.

Back down to earth
We cloudwalkers gently floated.
The grease of our harvest supper
Still upon empty mouths –
Terra firmly devoted.

The Bacchanalia was over -
Boozy God of derangement
Rent asunder: his goodness shared,
Blood into wine, flesh into bread.

*John Barleycorn is dead!*
*John Barleycorn is dead!*

The parched soil drank him dry:
The Goddess takes back what once was hers.

 *The power returns to the Mother,*
 *The power returns to the Mother.*


As we turned to the crimson-smeared day,
Imbibing the drunken sun,
Wetstone-slicked sickle in hand,


  Ready to make hay.

# AUTUMN EQUINOX

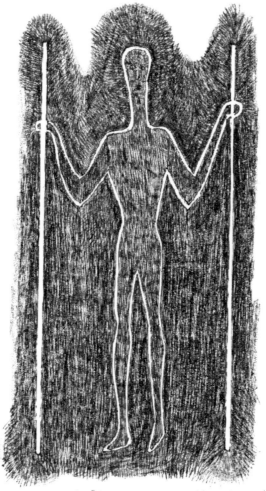

Long Man of Wilmington          Keron Armstrong

## SUMMER'S WAKE

The Earth is ablaze with flaming tears -
Shedded in grief as Her sun disappears.

For this is the time of the annual sunset,
When man must savour lest he forget.

A cauldron that tips its molten load –
As it touches the land, Midas glowed.

Reforging the world in a different vein,
Making us appreciate whatever will wane.

Leaves become gold to impress their presence –
Precious to us in their newfound transience.

Their weight, like their value, seems to have altered -
Heavy now they fall, as if indeed moulted.

Gravity and time take their toll,
Casting off weight in this seasonal cull.

The reaper scythes with relief –
Cutting the chaff from the wheatsheaf.

We reward our labours with indulgence,
Seducing our senses with Nature's opulence.

Her dark bounty tempts us to dine,
Enticed to sin on the fruits of the vine.

Its bouquet we judge as connoisseur –
Our tastes informing us of a good year.

The party is over, the revellers scattered,
The place where it was, in legacy, littered.

A lonely breeze comes to sweep it away -
The rest is absorbed in silent decay.

The garden is a film set deserted,
Yet still it is haunted by those departed.

Phantoms flicker of a glory past –
Images in sepia fading fast.

We thumb through the album but must let go –
Forgetting yesterday, remembering tomorrow.

As the evening arrives, our nostrils flare –
A season has passed, scenting night air.

The vessels absence still ripples make,

As we stand gently rocking in summer's wake.


The dying king sails to the Isle in rest

where he shall remain the Goddess' guest.


The holly resumes his thorny crown,

At his queen's side of blacker gown.


Briefly, the balance is maintained,

As we must gauged what has been gained.


Until the scales begin to sway,

And night takes over what once was day.


So rejoice! The year has come of age.

Our shadows stretching – like ink down the page.

# the enchantment of merlin

Like ivy to oak,

clinging, sapping,

Morgan overcame Merlin.


Yet the druid did not resist -

he had wearied of man's folly and pettiness.

His stratagem was implemented.

The pieces of the game were all in place.

Wood, water and air.


So, he caved into her

lips and eyes and hair.

By subtle voice and supple caress

he succumbed to the wiles of an enchantress.


Or was that how this legerdemain seemed to us?


What cruel love took place in that grove -

only the owl knows,

only the owl knows.


What ancient ritual was enacted

in spellbound Broceliande


where a magician was enchanted?

She stole the gramarye from the tip

of his tongue,

trapped him with his own cantrips.

Perhaps...


As water flowed the words of power.

She bathed in his spring,

drank his magic dry.

Leaving him wizened,

with bark skin and creaking limbs -

an old man in wood.


Fool!

She howled

a hollow victory.


Now Morgan held the keys to his mysteries,

but with them came responsibility.

The kingdom was in her

keeping.


Whilst the warlock was released

from mortal wheel.


He flowed through the roots of the land,

while le Fay was tied to Table Round,

bound by its deceptions and schemes.

As awake-walked

our sentinel oak seer,

guiding from afar -

Guardian of Britain;

Merlin's Enclosure

where Arthur dreams...

# CROWS IN THE WILLOWS

*Crows in the willows,*
*Toadstools in the grass,*
*Not like our love,*
*These things will pass.*

Be there snow on the furrow
Or sun on the dew,
Far weather foul,
I shall follow you.

Should moonlight shatter
On midnight lake
I shall never you forsake.

Should Spring uncoil
And Harvests fail,
You shall never hunger at all.

For I'll be always there for you,
Yes, I'll always care for you...

*Crows in the willows,*
*Toadstools in the grass,*
*Not like our love,*
*These things will pass.*

# SAMHAIN

# WILD HUNT

When mad mushrooms bloom
And dream mists still linger
Then restless souls will hear a horn
The call of Herne the Hunter.

He waits a forest threshold
Astride snorting stallion.
Garbed in skins,
Bow on back,
Bright-ringed horn in hand.
A crown of antlers upon his head –
King of the Wood, Herne.

His bestial huntsman gather
With their phantom pack.
The only sound a chorus of crows
Scattered by a second blast.

*The Wild Hunt Rides!*

Hoof beats shake dew from cobwebs,
Leave a whorl of bloody leaves.
They harrow the hollow lanes,
The old straight tracks,
Over hedge, through field,

Knowing no boundary,

Heeding not the law of the landgrabber.


Steed steaming,

Breath ragged,

You reach the edge of the grove

Where the quarry is cornered.

Dismounting,

Spear poised,

You close in for the kill.


Herne waits,

Arrow ready,

Aiming at you.

He shoots,

Then all around the baying of the

Gabriel Hounds

As they tear your soul to shreds.


First,

Wormfodder,

Earth turning,

Earth turning…

Then, reborn –

Robin in the berry bush,

Otter in the weir,

Owl scrying from her bowl,

Mouse hushed on wheat ear.

Red fox skulking at red dusk,

Bristled boar with deadly tusk.

Rutting stag of the Royal Tines,

*Rex Nemorensis,*

        Herne -

The Hunter

Became the hunted.

Animals are we all

So bless your beast

In time for the feast

And desecrators of the sacred wood

Beware!

When winter's tang

Sharpens our appetite

And the wild hunt rides!

# WOLF IN THE CITY

*There's a wolf loose in*
*the city*
*He's running through*
*my head*
*There's a wolf wild*
*within me*
*And I cannot get to bed.*

Tail swish
dream twitch
muffled bark
bolt awake!

Wolf opens his eyes
dark amber flashing
yawns as if to swallow
the sun
big tongue coiling
arcs his hackled back
claws tenterhook
withdraw

Wolf shakes his shaggy
mane of moonlight and
brimstone

sniffs the air with salt and pepper snout
and following his nose
he begins to prowl, with loping gait

A wolf is loose in the city tonight
all the traffic lights have stuck on amber
cars screech and swerve
                    to avoid the jaywalker

a red-eyed black beast
snapshot in headlights

a blur of fur against
the glass and steel
pad of leathery paws
on pavement running
through puddles of ink
writing his own lunatic tale
claws scratch on blank stone
searching for a meaning

There's a wolf loose in the city
wanting he knows not

until he finds it
just hunting hunting
with blind instinct
for a scratch for his itch
some heat for his bitch

wolf wants a moon to howl at
some this for his that
chasing tail, the right scent
loitering with intent

There's a wolf loose in the city
slipping into the skin of shadows
dark flash of silhouette slashing
alleyway, subway, dead-end street

stink marking
his neck of the woods
leaving his signature of animal graffiti
on corners and crossroads
wasteground and no-go zones

*There's a wolf loose in the city*
*He's running through my head*
*There's a wolf wild within me*
*And I cannot get to bed!*

# The Wicker Man

Fire in the heart, fire in the head -
Our wick is so short,
Long live the dead...
Torch my tinder, set me ablaze.
Divining sparks skyward rise.
Turn my lead into gold,
Alchemical treasures untold.
Tribal warmth, selfless light,
Dancing the darkness, waking the night.

I am the Wicker Man,
Burning up inside.
Hollow shell,
Nothing to hide.

I am the fuel of my own bonfire,
Let my life be my pyre.
Not to have lived fully
Is the only death.

I want to burn brighter
With my every breath.
Leave these wooden bones in a heap,
With wild flames I want to leap.

I am the wicker man,

Raise my cage to the ground,

Energy is never lost, it goes around.

Losing my skin, the infinite within.

Turning on the inside sun.

Shining brighter in the shadows,

And basking in the glow of the burning now.

# The BATTLE FOR The TREES

In the besieged glade
The horn-blast fades.
And the wood holds its breath.

Suddenly, a stirring of leaves -
Thunder of hooves on hollow road.
The horned one rides -
Herne has returned!

*Black dogs baying for blood,*
*Wild hunters in the wildwood.*
*Gathering the fallen,*
*Culling those who kill.*
*Outlaw and King's men*
*In death are equal.*

The gauntlet tightens its grip.
Overlord V underdog.
Iron ready, helmets down, jaws set:
Determined to destroy.

But thorns scratch, roots clutch,
Blind and block
From hew and hack.

*When will the axe no longer thirst?*
*When will the tall trees stop falling?*


Oak stands firm,

Willow bends,

Beech and hornbeam

The strong wind fends.

When it blows

The lesser boughs break.

Saplings trampled under foot.

Lives of many seasons topple.

Brief the flowering of warriors,

Flows the sap and blood.

Written in red the axe ogham.

White corpses in the green.


*Black dogs baying for blood,*
*Wild hunters in the wildwood.*
*Gathering the fallen,*
*Culling those who kill.*
*Outlaw and King's men*
*In death are equal.*


Crashing tree, clashing steel,

Blade bites wood, splinters bone.

Shattered, the peace of the grove.

A deadly toll, this mortal autumn.

Many-coloured mantles

Stripped from limbs.

Bare the arms that claw the air.


The cold wind keens,

Skeleton branches creak and whine.


Silence comes with the slain,

Mouths filled with earth.

Eyes gaze beyond,

Roots gape through wounds.

Rain cleans the battlefield of blood,

Enemies embrace the mud.


The wild hunt have reaped their harvest

But before they ride on

Their leader turns

To meet his son.

Dark eyes gaze deep,

Antlered head nods.


*The battle for the trees is won -*

*But not the war.*

*The wildwood will live on -*

*How long for?*


[From Robin of the Wildwood, with Fire Springs]

## HEATHER'S SPRING

There is a spring where hope does flow
-it's nearer than you think.

A place of peace and beauty
Where you can go to drink.

Upon a mossy bank
by a weeping bough
sit and spend some time
in the sacred now.

Listen to the gentle song,
which the waters sing.
Hearken to your heart,
the pulse of its beating.

Immerse and let the music
wash your woes away.
Heed the endless melody,
which the undines play.

Healing rings around you,
for all your ills a balm.
Waves of love enfold you
in an embrace so warm.

Let the love flow through you,
pouring from every pore.
Purifying you with truth,
the beauty that you are.

Thirsty, soul? Come taste
a draught of the infinite.
Baptise this body of water –
let it become light.

Pilgrim, this eternal source
shall always replenish.
Blessings of the circle,
return when you so wish.

Remember, all life flows
and will ever renew.
There is a spring where hope does flow
and it is inside you.

# WINTER SOLSTICE

Stoney Littleton Long Barrow                    Kevan Manwaring '99

# AWAKENING THE KING

Within the Spiral Castle
the sleeping King awaits,
awaits for the Grail of the Fool...

On the Axis of the Starry Wheel,
inside the Glassy Citadel,
at the Head of the Winding Stairs,
the Head of the Winding Stairs.

He Dreams
upon a bed of broken wings ~
an Icarus sunset he fell
( and so must surely rise again )

*Bright King Awake Within.*

From a gleam in the eye of night
to a star on the brow of day;

rise and shine
spark to pyre
pentagram, man
breath to fire!

Phoenix,

return to the ashes of thy Resurrection.

To the Sacred Spring

where once you bathed as leprous swineherd

to emerge a King.

*Bright King Awake Within.*

Angle of Bath I invoke thee.

Many-feathered Man-God I know thy name:

*Bladud.*

Bladud; father of Lear, son of Hudibras -

descended from Trojan Aeneas.

Bladud; temple-builder, necromancer -

raise thyself from the dead.

Bladud; mathematician, magician –

teach us your wisdom.

Bladud ; Arch-Druid, oak amongst men –

Open thy seer eyes,

Shake the snakes from thy hair,

Stretch mighty limbs,

Spread mended wings

And soar!


Down to us souls,

To restore that which restored you –

The Shrine of Sulis.


*Bright King Awake Within.*

# The PROPhETS OF LOS

Listen to the Prophets of Los…
Magicians of the Imagination,
of eternal voice, of infinite vision,
We chant the dream into reality,
Divine omens of other worlds,
Pulling the sword from the words,
Awaken the Monarch in the many.


Listen to the Prophets of Los…
To the bounty of abandonment,
The freedom of the fearless,
The discoveries of the lost.
Finding the healing in painful lessons,
The wisdom of past mistakes.
What lives of brilliant failure!


Listen to the Prophets of Los…
To blow it all in one night,
In wild acts of pure art.
To liberate the Shining City,
To burn with a stolen fire,
To cry with the wolf,
Losing oneself in a deeper wonder.

Listen to the Prophets of Los…

Drinking to the brim,

Dancing on the brink,

Leaping into the dark.

Trembling power, breathless roar.

Let the immovable mountain

come to the irresistible shore.


Listen to the Prophets of Los…

Give me a temple of communion

With a company of the heart.

What new worlds we could create!

What dreams forged out of the manacles of day.

Usurping control from the fat conspirators.

And with fiery bow storming tomorrow.


Listen, listen!

O invisible brotherhood,

Sisters of mystery,

Bonded by breath and blood.


Release the energy of unrealised desires,

Of forgotten destinies.

Resolve into action

The yearnings of our yesterdays.

Planting the frail flag of our hopes

On the heights of aspiration,

Where another world is possible,

The present not wasted, the Prophets honoured.

Glastonbury Tor

Kevan Manwaring/99

## SUDRISE PRAISE

Thank you,
Mother Earth,
For holding me in your arms all night
And bringing me back to a world of light.

Thank you, Father Sun,
For returning to brighten our day,
May you shine for us
And show us the way.

Thank you, Brothers and Sisters,
Of water, earth, wood and air.
I shall tread lightly
on this planet we share.

Thank you, Great Mystery.
May we live this day with the wisdom of love,
Guided by the blessings of
below and above.

May peace prevail on Earth
And in all our hearts.
Love and light to our loved ones
Wherever they may be.

*So Mote It Be.*

# THE SHINING WORD

'He who gives no light will never be a star'

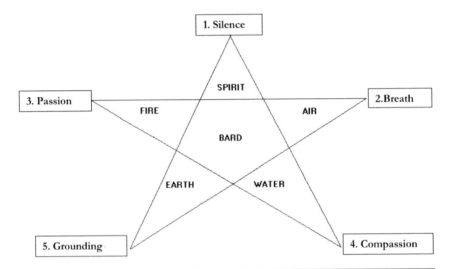

1. Silence

SPIRIT

3. Passion

FIRE

AIR

2. Breath

BARD

EARTH

WATER

5. Grounding

4. Compassion

1. **Silence.** Listen to your heart, to the Earth, to Spirit, to the Universe. What does it want you to say? Meditate. Invoke the Awen & ask for inspiration. Consider the Endless Sound: the silence between the words.

2. **Breath.** Breathe from below (diaphragm).Warm-up the vocal chords with voice exercises, eg humming, toning, chanting. Deep breaths to relax and to keep your lungs filled. Speak slowly and clearly. Project.

3. **Fire in the Heart.** Speak from the heart and say it loud and proud, with passion, with sincerity, with energy, but do not 'scorch' – temper with…

4. **Ripples in the pond.** After passion comes compassion. Be sensitive to your audience, your words and yourself. Imagine dropping pebbles in a pond with your words – let each one have its impact. Be aware of the energy you are raising/atmosphere you are creating.

5. **Bringing it down to earth.** Make sure your message reaches home by manifesting it fully. Use body language, movement, props, costume, drums. Establish and use the space. Use humour and spontaneity. Take the audience on a magical healing journey there and back again.

# BARÒic peRfORMADCE Cips

1. Find the fire in your head – the spark to set the poem alight. What inspires you? Your enthusiasm will shine through.
2. Use rhyme, rhythm, imagery and alliteration as mnemonic devices.
3. Say it out loud until it 'scans to the ear.'
4. Consider what is the core emotion or message. Does it come across?
5. Keep it simple – complication leads to alienation. Be clever between the lines. Communication is about being understood – it's up to you.
6. Listen to the audience. Let the silences speak.
7. Remember the effort spent crafting your words – don't throw them away. Speak them with respect. Say them like they're newly-minted.
8. Don't undersell yourself, apologise or mumble your words.
9. Keep pre-ambles to a minimum. Cut out altogether if possible. Go in with a bang!
10. Look sharp & sound sharp. Dress to impress. Wear your 'confidence overcoat'.
11. Remember to breathe! Don't speak too fast…Pause…Let the audience in.
12. Make eye contact as much as possible.
13. Learn your words off by hear -it's more entertaining and more impressive. Audiences appreciate the time and effort spent learning your words.
14. Passion transcends ability, but honing your craft can only help.
15. Sincerity shines through. Take your efforts seriously and others will to, but humour wins over an audience, circumvents the hecklers and criticisms of pretension.
16. Use body language consciously. Practise your stage presence.
17. If you use a persona still be fully present and real.
18. Get there early. Practise in space if possible. Warm-up voice before.
19. Practise with microphone if using a PA, or projecting if not. Sound check.
20. Use the performance space. Be aware of energy of room/audience.
21. Performing poetry is a buzz – enjoy it. Stand up there and shine!

## WAY OF AWEN DEVELOPMENT

### YEAR-LONG BARDIC TRAINING ROGRAMME

With storyteller, performance poet, author & teacher Tallyessin aka Kevan Manwaring, MA Teaching & Practise of Creative Writing, Cardiff University. Winner of the Bardic Chair of Bath, & member of Fire Springs (Arthur's Dream, Robin of the Wildwood)

2004 dates

**Voice of the Sea, Imbolc - February 13, 14, 15**
Introduction to The Bardic Tradition and the Mystery School of Taliesin, at Morlais, Borth, Cardigan Bay. Finding inspiration. Writing & sharing poems of the sea & season. Celebration in honour of Brighid, Ceridwen. Initiation at Bedd Taliesin. 4 miles of beach. Waterfalls & wildfowl wetlands. Stunning views of Snowdonia.

**Voice of the Wind, Spring Equinox - March 19, 20, 21**
Learn the craft of the Windsmith, working with breath, voice, and the element of air. Walking between the worlds. Visit the famous chalk giant - the Long Man of Wilmington on the South Downs. Stay at Alfriston YHA. Join Gorsedd of Anderida for ceremony at Long Man, & celebration in The Giant's Rest pub.

**Voice of the Fire, Beltane – April 30, May 1, 2**
Kindling the Fire in the Head. YHA Blackboys woodland hostel., E. Sussex. Belfire/Beltain celebration. Put passion into your performance & leap the flames of desire! Enjoy the Jack-in-the Green Festival, May Day, Hastings.

**Voice of the Sun, Summer Solstice – June 18, 19, 20, 21, 22**
Celebrate the solstice & work with circles/light in stunning Cornish coastal campsite. Gorsedd at Boscawen-Un ring. Sun, sea, sand & stone circles. Bonhomie & sunbathing. Enjoy Mazey Day at the Golowan Festival, Penzance. Reconnect with the source.

**Voice of Earth, Lughnasadh – July 31, August 1, 2**
Beginning of harvest. Exploring Avebury. Visit Windmill Hill, the Avenue, Silbury Hill & West Kennet Long Barrow. Camping at the Barge Inn, Vale of Pewsey (crop circle central), next to Kennet & Avon canal. Close to Wansdyke, Knap Hill & Adam's Grave.

## Voice of the Trees, Autumn Equinox – Sept 17, 18, 19

Explore the ways of the Wildwood at Rocks East Woodland, near Bath. Magical 100 acre woodland with sculpture/poetry trails, grotto, druid stones, Celtic Tree Wheel, miz-maze. Celebrate the Autumn Equinox, exploring its meaning to you. Camping with facilities.

## Voice of the Ancestors, Samhain – October 29, 30, 31

Honouring the ancestors. Avalon, Isle of the Dead. Visit Tor, Chalice Well etc. Sunday - Samhain Fair: Peat Moors visitor centre - Competition for the Bard of the Avalon Marshes. Watch the burning of the Wicker Man! Staying at Glastonbury, Backpackers Hostel.

## Voice of the Stars, Winter Solstice - Dec 17, 18, 19

Cycles, prophecy, stardom. Persona & repertoire. Visit to Solsbury Hill & Stoney Littleton Long Barrow. Stargazing from The Bridge of Stars. Stay at the White Hart hostel in Bath. Participate in a WOAD Bardic Showcase as part of the Bardic Festival of Bath. Awarding of bardic honours in Gorsedd of Caer Badon Watch the Battle of the Bards for the Bardic Chair of Bath.

Each bardic weekend is £150-75 (pay what you can afford). Includes full board & accommodation (except on campsites). Maximum 12 participants. Minimum 4. Cheques made payable to 'Tallyessin'. Send SAE to The Cauldron, 7 Dunsford Place, Bath BA2 6HF. FFI Kevan Tel:01225 3340204

WOAD participants at Bedd Taliesin, Feb 2004

Titles from Awen Publications

/ | \

# WRITING THE LAND

## An Anthology of Natural Words

EDITED BY KEVAN MANWARING

WINNER OF A

READING FAMILIES MILLENNIUM AWARD

Lovers of nature will enjoy this diverse collection of poetry and prose. Within these pages you will find pieces on wildlife, trees, water, earth, light, places, travel, memory and time. They range from the funny to the profound, the down-to-earth to the spiritual. Informative, but never preaching, these are words to be enjoyed. Dip into this anthology for relaxation, companionship and inspiration.

£5 ISBN: 0-9546137-0-8 All proceeds go to Friends of the Earth

To order ring:01225 334204

/|\

# Fire in the head

Creative Process in the Celtic Diaspora

By Kevan Manwaring

In this erudite and engaging work Kevan Manwaring MA, winner of the Bardic Chair of Caer Badon (Bath), explores the fascinating process of creativity in Celtic poetry, looking at a wide-range of poets across the Celtic diaspora. WB Yeats' 'Song of Wandering Aengus' is looked at in detail as a working model of the creative process and poetic initiation. A poet himself, the author approaches the massive corpus of material with a bardic sensibility and insight, being a lyrical a reliable guide across the Celtic threshold into the Otherworld of the imagination and inspiration.

Awen Publications   ISBN: 0-95646137-2-4   Price £5   112pp

# /|\

# SPEAK LIKE RAIN

## LETTERS TO A YOUNG BARD

### By Kevan Manwaring

## *Awaken the Bard Within!*

This series of letters are based upon the Shining Word workshops designed to awaken the bard within – taking the poet from page to stage. Inspired by Rainer Maria Rilke's 'Letters to a Young Poet' they are written to Kevan's earlier self of 12 years ago (when he began to write and perform poetry) in an informal style, but with the benefit of hard-won experience, humility and humanity. Techniques in composition and performance are shared between initiate and novice in an easy-to-follow 5 point method: useful for anyone who wishes to walk the bardic path, craft their words for ceremony and celebration, and shine.

106 | Awen Publications    ISBN: 0-9546137-1-6   Only £3    56pp booklet

### COMING SOON FROM AWEN!

# BARÖIC
# ŊANÖBOOK

## BY
## KEVAN MANWARING

Bringing together Speak Like Rain & Fire in the Head in one volume with exercises and other essays. All you need to begin your bardic path in one book! The official Way Of Awen Development Coursebook.

## CONTENTS

1. Foreword
2. Introduction
3. Starting Out
4. Mouth to Mouth - The Bardic Tradition
5. Fire in the Head – creative process in the Celtic diaspora
6. Speak like Rain – letters to a young bard, incl. performance tips.
7. The Way of Awen: the Bardic Year (festivals & exercises)
8. Voice of the Sea - Imbolc
9. Voice of the Wind – Spring Equinox
10. Voice of the Fire – Beltane
11. Voice of the Sun – Summer Solstice
12. Voice of the Earth – Lughnasadh
13. Voice of the Trees – Autumn Equinox
14. Voice of the Ancestors – Samhain
15. Voice of the Stars – Winter Solstice
16. Conclusion
17. Bibligraphy/suggested reading
18. Contacts: WOAD, Druid Orders & other organisations.

£9 ISBN 0-9546137-4-0
Reserve your copy now from Awen Publications!
Tel: 01225 334204
AVAILABLE SPRING 2005

# TALLYESSIN
## WINNER OF THE
## BARDIC CHAIR OF BATH
M.A Teaching & Practise of Creative Writing
*Behold the Shining Brow*
*Forge the Shining Word*

Photograph by Helen Murray 1999